Edle Catharina Norman

Beautiful Winter

Contents

First published in 2007 as
Vintervakkert - Kranser og Dekorasjoner
by Edle Catharina Norman
copyright 2007 © Cappelen Damm AS

Published by Sellers Publishing, Inc.
English translation copyright © 2012 Sellers Publishing, Inc.
All rights reserved.

Translation by Margaret Berge Hartge

Sellers Publishing, Inc.
161 John Roberts Road, South Portland, Maine 04106
Visit our Web site: www.sellerspublishing.com
E-mail: rsp@rsvp.com

ISBN 13: 978-1-4162-0847-1
e-ISBN: 978-1-4162-0858-7
Library of Congress Control Number: 2012931284

10 9 8 7 6 5 4 3 2 1

Printed and bound in China

Foreword

After my first book, *Beautiful Wildflowers,* was published, I received an unbelievable amount of lovely comments, both from people I knew and strangers, who said that the book opened their eyes to all the beauty that surrounds us in nature. Many became inspired to make their own small masterpieces with wildflowers and other natural materials. It is always a joy for an author to receive such wonderful responses to his or her work. In my flower studio, I often get requests and commissions that challenge my creativity. Consequently, I am always developing my own techniques and utilizing new materials. I love sharing my ideas with others, so when my publisher encouraged me to write a new book, with an emphasis on decorations for the fall, Christmas, and winter, I was ready for the challenge.

Beautiful Winter: Holiday Wreaths, Garlands & Decorations for Your Home & Table is different from my first book, since wildflowers, naturally, are not used in winter decorations. In this book, I have emphasized the use of natural materials that are available throughout the fall and winter seasons, and shapes and colors that fit with winter's mood. Together with these materials from nature's own treasure chest, I have used flowers and seasonal greenery that can be bought at florist shops throughout the country.

I hope that this book will inspire you to make unique arrangements from all the beauty that nature gives us. Beautiful decorations convey moods and atmospheres for everyday life as well as for the holiday seasons. If you exchange the typical Christmas flowers with seasonal flowers, you can create entirely different expressions fitting for any time of the year.

Good luck!

Tools & Equipment

Knife

The knife must always be sharp. Use it to cut flower stems cleanly. This is necessary to achieve maximum water absorption and flower durability.

Wire cutters

Small wire cutters are a must for cutting the floral wires and many other things.

Rose shears are useful for cutting branches from birch, juniper, or other materials with woody stems.

Pliers

Pliers are practical for cutting thicker wires. You can also use them for twisting two or more floral wires together.

Drill

An electric drill is nice for making holes in chestnuts, cork fungi, bark, roots, etc.

Floral wire

Floral wire in different lengths and thicknesses is used to fasten conifer cones, chestnuts, cork fungi, rose hips, etc. to the decorations. It can also be used to make shapes for wreaths and other design ideas. We even make our own greening pins by bending short floral wires, which are cut to a point at each end. I only use unvarnished wire.

Floral tape

This elastic tape can sometimes be wrapped around floral wire. Stretch the tape while you are wrapping and overlapping it. This tape gets sticky from the warmth of your hands.

Spool wire

Thicker than stem wire, spool wire comes on a spool and is used for wrapping wreaths, making metal constructions, tying branches together, etc. I prefer to use the unvarnished wire. Copper-, silver-, or gold-colored wires can give a festive feel to holiday decorations.

Stem wire

This also comes on a spool, but stem wire is thinner and is used for wrapping lichen and moss. We also use it to tie thin twigs together. It is available in many colors.

Other tools

In addition to the above-mentioned tools, you may need a tape measure, rope, hot-glue gun and glue sticks, a glue pan, etc.

All tools can be bought primarily at hardware stores, floral shops, or craft and hobby stores.

Test tubes

These are made from transparent glass and can be purchased in many different sizes. They are attached to the decoration or small tree branch with stem wire or spool wire. You can let the glass be visible in the decoration if you wish.

Plastic "test tubes" with rubber tops

These plastic flower tubes are not meant to show in the decorations. They can be purchased in craft stores and at some floral shops.

Markers

Light-colored cuts on branches can be concealed with markers, if the light-colored cut surface is not a part of the design.

Chlorine wash

Be sure to rinse all vases and glass containers in chlorinated water to kill bacteria.

Floral foam

I use floral foam for many projects, as it's very versatile. It can be used in fresh-flower arranging and as a pinning mass for other projects. A wet floral foam is good for extending the life of freshly cut greens used in decoration, but it can only be used once. The foam is easily found at craft stores or floral shops, and part of its popularity is that it's available in many shapes: balls, wreaths, bars, cones, etc. Cut the size you need and place it in water; it will sink, and after a few minutes, it will be ready to use.

A dry floral foam is used in decorations with dry materials that are pinned or glued on.

Materials

Let yourself be lured outside and experience nature's own treasure chest. In the fall, fill bags with rich raw materials for winter decorations, before snow conceals all the treasures, and moisture ruins their color. There is an unbelievable amount of decorative materials to be found: Lichen of different colors and shapes. Pillow moss and flat moss. Chestnuts and chestnut husks. Beech husks and oak husks. Conifer cones in all sizes and shapes — for example, alder, hemlock, different spruces, larch, pine, eastern white pine, and fir. Corky fungi. Bark. Roots and twigs. Feathers and beautiful stones.

Treatment

To extend the durability of natural materials — all of which contain moisture — they must be dried before storage or use, otherwise they will rot. Air-dry them on newspapers. Materials which may contain insects — for example, cork fungi and half-rotten bark — can be treated in the oven using low temperatures. Check frequently.

Storage

Store smaller natural materials in plastic produce containers with lids. They have a nice size, are airy, and can be stacked so they require little space. Very small materials can be stored in glass containers and jars.

Store-bought materials

If you are short on time and cannot go gathering natural materials in forests, fields, and mountains, you can buy many of the materials at hobby stores or from florists.

Natural Elements I Love

- Corky fungi (polyporaceae): I call these tree mushrooms, as they typically grow on trees or fallen limbs in the forest
- Chestnuts
- Chestnut husks: this is the spiky "case" that chestnuts grow in; great texture and shape, they are perfect for seasonal projects that are used over and over.
- Lichen: remove from the plant it's been growing on and air dry for several days. Lichen is a great addition to a wreath, with its straight-from-nature texture and varying shades of green
- Club moss: is a wonderful addition, with interesting- looking foliage; try gathering it in small "bouquets."

elpful Information

hieve the best possible result, the following
nation maybe useful:

w to tie two branches together

When a project calls for
attaching one branch to
another, I recommend using
a continuous length of spool
wire for both branches.
Wrap the spool wire around
ranch 2 to 3 times. Secure it in place by twisting
vo ends tightly around each other. Take the
branch and wrap the wire 2 to 3 times around
d lock by twisting the wire ends the same way as
e. The branches will not come apart this way, and
ionally, it looks a lot better than if you wrap the
around both branches at the same time. Do not
ie wires before your project is done! You might
to tie another branch to the same spot.

ening the branches

Often it is necessary to soften
branches — especially any
thick ends — for easier shaping
in twig decorations. See the
accompanying photograph:
Hold your hands around the
branch, closely together, with
humb beside the other. Bend the branch by

moving the hands carefully away from each other
without loosening your grip — you may want to wear
gloves. Move your hands up along the entire branch,
bending as you go. Start from the beginning again,
and continue until the branch is pliable and soft. If you
cheat on this process, you risk breaking the branch.

Wire pinning

Chestnuts can be pinned
(or attached to a piece) by
drilling a hole in the nut,
dipping a short, stiff floral
wire about 1¼–1½ inches
long sparingly into glue and
pushing it quickly through
the hole in the chestnut.

But if you pin them while they are fresh, you can avoid
drilling and push the floral wire (it must be cut with a
point) through the skin without drilling. The wire will
attach better this way than if you only glue it on.

Coniferous cones are pinned with stiff floral wire
which is wrapped a couple of times around, near
the bottom of the cones. Twist the wire ends tightly
together, wrapping toward the bottom.

Mushrooms and other fungi that are characterized by
a corky, hard surface are pinned by drilling two holes
through the edge on the back (see photograph above).
Thread a stiff floral wire through each hole and bend
the wire ends toward each other.

9

Wreaths

evergreen Holiday Wreath

This chubby, green wreath of blue spruce, noble fir, yew, and cedar looks good hanging on an exterior door when the snow is falling and the holidays are approaching. In this example, it is decorated with laurel leaves and berries.

Instructions

* Cut evergreen branches into short, pretty pieces.
* Attach the spool wire to the straw wreath.
* Place many small sprigs in a circle beside each other on top of the wreath, from the outside to the inside, and wrap the wire around the wreath and the branches.
* Continue to place new branches partially on top of each other and wrap the wire around them.
* Build up larger or smaller areas with the same type of evergreens.

Materials

* straw wreath form
* spool wire or greening pins
* different types of evergreen branches — for example, noble fir, spruce, juniper, yew, and cedar
* lichen, pinecones, lichen twigs, rose hips, laurel leaves with berries

Tips

Instead of spool wire, you can fasten the materials to the straw wreath with greening pins. When doing this, you can use longer twigs.

You can decorate the wreath with lichen, pinecones, lichen twigs, rose hips, berries, etc.

13

Traditional Pine Wreath

Materials

* chubby pine branches
* straw wreath form
* spool wire or greening pins
* pinecones

You can make a solid and delightfully chubby wreath from lush pine branches and a variety of pinecones. Hang it on a front door, or (as pictured) on an ornamental wrought-iron railing. Guests will begin to feel the Christmas spirit on their way into your home.

Instructions

* Cut up the pine branches into short pieces.
* Fasten the spool wire around the straw wreath form.
* Place many sprigs in a circle next to each other, working from the outside to the inside of the wreath, and fasten them with spool wire.
* Place a new round of sprigs partially on top of the others and fasten them.
* When the wreath is covered with pine sprigs, which all lie in the same direction, fasten the pinecones to the wreath. Pin the pinecones as shown on page 9.

Natural Elements Wreath

This is the kind of wreath you can use the entire year. It can hang on the wall or over a fireplace mantel as an everyday decoration. As the holidays approach, you can add candleholders and use it on the table as an advent wreath (see page 41). Or you can decorate it with red berries and rose hips and hang it on the door as an inviting ornament that will enhance the holiday spirit.

Instructions

* Attach a loop of spool wire to the straw form for hanging.
* Pin (see page 9) the tree mushrooms, chestnuts, and larger pinecones. Begin to add them to the straw form either following the design in the accompanying photograph or your own pattern.
* Use hot glue to attach most of the smaller cones, lichen, club moss, and chestnut husks.
* Place remaining lichen and moss in areas where the straw form is showing through.

Tips

Make sure the materials cover the straw wreath form completely, both on the inside and the outside, all the way to the work surface.

All materials must be completely dry, or they will rot.

Any heavy materials that have not been pinned should be attached with greening pins.

Materials

* straw wreath form
* corky fungi
* chestnuts
* chestnut husks
* lichen
* club moss
* hot-glue gun and glue sticks
* greening pins
* spool wire
* 4 candleholders (or a wire-frame advent wreath with candleholders), optional
* pinecones

Pinecone & Chestnut Wreath

A walk in the woods on a beautiful autumn day will provide all the materials you'll need for this wreath. Pick the chestnuts as soon as they fall off the trees. Don't forget to grab the husks (for other projects) and pick club moss for a vibrant green dash of color in between the cones. You can pick pinecones all year round.

Instructions

* Fasten the spool wire around the wreath form, and make a loop on the back side, which allows you to hang up the wreath.
* Prepare all pinecones and chestnuts with wires beforehand, as explained on page 9.
* Compose a pattern where you group the materials in larger patches. Attach small bouquets of club moss with greening pins between the pinecones. You can push lichen between the chestnuts.
* When done, decorate the wreath with red twig dogwood branches. Push the thicker end directly into the wreath and attach the thinner end with greening pins.

Materials
* straw wreath form, preferably covered with moss (Be sure to thoroughly dry moss before covering.)
* pinecones
* chestnuts
* chestnut husks
* lichen
* club moss
* greening pins
* branches of red twig dogwood or similar shrub
* spool wire

Bark Wreath with Roses

Bark beetles ruin many trees, but even their damage can yield something beautiful. On the inside of the bark from such stricken trees, the beetles will have made an exciting pattern of veins in the brown surface. A wreath made from such unusual, raw pieces of bark can be a contrasting frame around refined and glowing roses. Here the roses are surrounded by lichen.

Instructions

* Drill two small holes beside each other in the bark, thread floral wire through the holes, and tie the ends of the wires around the metal wreath form or ring at the bottom. Each piece of bark is attached in this way in two places.
* Place the pieces of bark so they overlap, and use hot glue to secure them in place.
* Place the finished bark wreath at the outer edges of the platter, place floral foam in the center, and decorate it with flowers and natural materials.

Mistletoe Wreath

Mistletoe is part of the tradition of Christmas. In the olden days, people believed that it kept witches, demons, and illness at bay. In addition, it was considered good luck for a couple to kiss under a bunch of mistletoe. Why don't we stimulate love a little further at the holidays by making a heart or a wreath of mistletoe?

Materials for the wreath

* a bunch of mistletoe
* a stiff metal ring or thick spool wire
* floral wire
* floral tape

Instructions

* Attach mistletoe branches to the ring with floral wire, with a minimum of two attachments per branch.
* Attach them more or less frequently, depending upon how transparent or dense you want the wreath.
* If you are using thick spool wire to make the wreath, you should wrap several wires over each other so the metal ring becomes stiff. Afterwards you can cover the wire with floral tape if you wish to conceal it.
* To make the heart-shaped wreath, follow the same instructions for the wreath, except you should form a heart from the ring.

Materials for the heart

* a bunch of mistletoe
* a stiff heart formed by a metal frame or thick spool wire
* floral wire
* floral tape

Juniper Heart

Juniper branches are light and airy, and they present a soft yet textural silhouette. They are a good choice for this sweet, modest heart.

Materials

* juniper branches
* thick floral wire
* spool wire

Instructions

* Attach several lengths of spool wire together and form a heart.
* Wrap additional floral wire around the heart shape to make it more stable.
* Attach juniper branches with floral wire as close together or as sparsely as you like, depending upon how you want the heart to appear.

Tips

You get a more interesting heart shape if you bend the bottom point a little to the side.

Birch Heart with Berries

If you have any birch trees close by, you will never be short of materials for a variety of charming wreaths and decorations. The strong and flexible branches are easy to work with, and a heart featuring rose hips is a different kind of wreath that will brighten your home both at Christmas and throughout the winter.

Instructions

* Soften birch branches as described on page 9.
* Form a heart using many branches. The number of branches you use depends on how chubby you wish the heart to be. Attach the branches to each other with stem wire.
* To make the rose hip vine, wrap stem wire tightly around the small rose hip stem a few times. As you make the vine release the stem wire from the spool little by little, and wrap with even spaces between the rose hip stems.
* Wrap the rose hip vine around the heart, and decorate with some fresh greenery — for example, club moss.

Materials

* birch branches
* rose hips
* spool wire
* stem wire
* greenery for decoration

Tips

You can make the rose hip vine at the same time as you are wrapping it around the birch heart.

Tear-Shaped Twig Wreath

With tough, pliable birch branches you can make all kinds of wreath variations. Here I have fashioned a tear-shaped wreath with a wide bottom, where you can place fresh flowers. This is quite a different look, and you can, of course, decorate the wreath with dry materials instead.

Instructions

* Make a ring of two birch branches by tying the thicker ends at the top and the thinner ends at the bottom with spool wire. Attach more branches, with the thickest part at the top.
* Attempt to "straighten out" the ring at the bottom by attaching some stronger branches horizontally.
* Attach some thin branches at the bottom to increase the volume.
* Choose whatever natural materials you wish for the base of the wreath. Attach with spool wire or stem wire, depending upon the weight of the material. After you've finished, place flowers in water holders (see page 7) on the bottom of the wreath, and cover the holders with lichen or moss.

Tips

The wreath should be light at the top and heavy at the bottom. However, the overall impression should be transparent.

Materials

* birch branches
* spool wire
* stem wire
* lichen, moss, pinecones, bark, etc.
* flowers in small water holders with rubber tops

Hawthorn Wreath

The twigs of older hawthorn trees — members of the rose family — make great wreaths. With their lichen-coated branches, they are so beautiful by themselves that you almost don't have to decorate them at all!

Instructions

* Tie the small branches to a metal ring with stem wire. Each small branch must be fastened at least twice.
* When the wreath is as dense as you want it, you can decorate with some small larch cones.

Tips

This wreath can be hung in a window or on a wall. You can also attach four strings to it and hang it horizontally with small Christmas lights attached.

Materials

* a metal ring, or several lengths of spool wire bunched together and formed into a stiff ring
* hawthorn branches or similar
* larch cones or other decorations
* stem wire
* spool wire

Materials

* pliable birch branches, ready-made wire wreath form, or spool wire
* red and yellow stems from the red twig dogwood shrub
* chestnut or beech husks, small pinecones, lichen, feathers, and berries
* stem wire
* a drill or a hot-glue gun and glue sticks

A small wreath made with the bright red and yellow twigs from dogwood shrubs is eye catching in winter. Simply adorned with pinecones, chestnut or beech husks, berries, lichen, and even feathers, it brings a jewel-like sensibility to any home interior.

Instructions

* There are a few options for shaping the wreath and attaching the decorative elements: a ready-made wire wreath form, create your own ring using spool wire, or simply using pliable birch twigs to shape the wreath.
* Attach one or more each of the red and yellow branches from the dogwood shrub to the ring. Use spool or stem wire, depending on the tension in the branch.
* Now you can attach different materials to the wreath. Island lichen gives a transparent effect. Husks from a chestnut tree are attached to the wreath with stem wire, which is pulled through two holes at the bottom of the husk. Use a drill with the smallest bit. Or, use small dabs of hot glue. Tiny alder cones are very decorative. Feathers make the wreath elegant.

Tips

Save small, oval rose hips during fall. They will give the wreath a warm and beautiful glow. Here I have used shiny, red berries from the barberry bush.

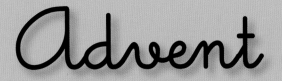

Advent

Advent Table Wreath

Larch trees can be found growing in North America, from the mountains of Virginia north to Hudson Bay and across New England. They also grow in the U.K. and Europe. For this wreath, I used the long, fresh branches of younger larch shoots — some with the cones still attached. The wreath is decorated with five beautiful purple orchids. I suggest making the wreath deep, so that plastic water tubes with rubber tops (see page 7) can be inserted and used to prolong the life of the flowers.

Instructions

* Make a ring of birch branches.
* Fasten larch branches to the birch ring with spool wire, and attach layer upon layer of larch branches to increase depth and width.
* Eventually, you can slip additional larch branches in between the branches that are already tied to the wreath, attaching them with stem wire in just a few places.
* Place water tubes in the wreath and decorate with flowers.

Tips

Large flower heads lying on the wreath look good. However, you can also use flowers with longer stems.

Materials

* fresh larch branches
* some birch branches
* spool wire
* stem wire
* test tubes
* flowers

Materials

* birch branches
* spool wire
* stem wire
* rope and string
* clip-on candleholders
* nice wrapping paper
* gold numbers

Tips

It is an advantage if
the branches are long.
The wreath must have
a certain depth, so
you will need quite
a few. Use clip-on
candleholders if you
wish to add candles to
the wreath.

A solid wreath of birch branches can function very well as a hanging Advent calendar. Attach 24 small, nicely wrapped surprises to the underside. When Advent is over, the wreath can be used for other occasions.

Instructions

* Soften the branches as described on page 9.
* Start with one branch, make a circle as large as desired, and wrap the crossing point with spool wire as described on page 9. The rest of the main branch should be attached at one or more places on this ring. Start with long spool wires so that you can use them to continuously attach new branches, which are placed on top of each other.
* Attach a new branch to the underlying branch at a new spot. Attach many new branches in the same manner by establishing several points of attachment. Later, attach side branches to these crossing points or new points of attachment, either with spool wire or stem wire (for the thinnest branches). Slip the thickest part of the branch through the underlying branches until it meets the layer beneath. In this way, you can continue to attach new branches to the wreath. Make sure to create nice bow shapes, and do not attach the branch at too many points.
* Attach four thin, double ropes to the wreath for hanging, and collect them in a knot a distance from the wreath.
* Attach hooks made from floral wire to the underside of the wreath, so the packages can easily be hung and removed from the wreath.
* Either write the dates on the packages or use small, self-adhesive numbers from a craft store. Make sure to spread the dates so that the wreath does not hang crooked when packages are removed.

Advent Wreath with Candles

Often, the ideal time to collect the basic materials for wreath making is after a storm. The wind can blow those hard-to-reach branches laden with cones right at your feet. This design uses larch cones, but any small-size cones from a white pine or a lodgepole pine will work. Here I have decorated with hemp rope, small lingonberry twigs for a spot of green, and four advent candles.

Instructions

* Make a ring using several lengths of spool wire. Twist double wires to make the ring stiff enough.
* Divide the larch branches into short lengths, and fasten one small twig after the other to the ring with stem wire. Attach them in such a manner that the wreath becomes the size you desire.
* Make a loop in the wreath with spool wire in case you want to hang it on the wall or on a door.
* Place four candleholders with long spikes into the wreath.
* Decorate with ropes or other objects.

Tips

Make sure that the stem wire wraps toward the branches, so that it is not visible on the larch cones.

If you want to further decorate the wreath, you can slip a little lichen between the larch cones.

Materials

* approx 75–80 larch cones on branches
* spool wire
* stem wire
* hemp rope
* 4 candles & small holders
* winter greens

41

Advent Log with Candle

Materials

* one bent log
* drill
* evergreen decorations
* candles
* thick aluminum foil
* hot-glue gun and
  glue sticks
* hammer and nails

Anything you can attach candles or candleholders to
can be used as an Advent candlestick. A piece of a birch
branch or trunk or another tree will work wonderfully.
Here I have decorated the birch log with noble spruce.
Simple, but effective.

Instructions

* Cut an adequate piece from the tree.
* Cut parts of the underside off to make the candlestick
  log lie stable on the table.
* Drill four large holes in the log, sized to fit the candles
  you are using.
* Cover the holes with thick aluminum foil and place the
  candles inside.
* Decorate the candlestick log with evergreens that
  are attached with hot glue or with small nails that are
  pounded into the log with a hammer.

Tips

Alternatively, you can drill smaller holes into the log and
stick a candleholder with a spike into each hole.

Materials

* branches from evergreens
* spool wire
* medium-weight floral wire
* decorations like spruce cones in assorted types and sizes
* strings of small electric lights (optional)

Garland

Short, long. Narrow, wide. Hanging or lying. With or without lights. With or without decorations. With sprigs of spruce, fir, juniper, or other evergreens, individually or combined — the possibilities for decorations are limitless. Around the entry door, on the wall, on a table, or along a railing, a garland creates good, old-fashioned holiday spirit. Here you can see a fir garland that is fastened to a stair railing. It is simply decorated with pinecones.

Instructions

* Cut side branches off the main branches if you want a narrow garland, or use the whole branch if the garland is to be wide and large.
* Place one branch partially on top of another and tie them together with spool wire. Place new branches on top, but displaced in relationship to each other. Wrap. Make sure that the spool wire only wraps around the main branch and does not squish the side branches.
* A large and heavy garland that is going to be hanging must be secured to prevent it from unraveling. Tie floral wire tightly around the main branch, at different points with even spacing.
* The end of the garland should be hidden with sprigs which are wrapped in the opposite direction.
* You can decorate a garland made from spruce with spruce cones, and one made of pine with pinecones.

On page 69 you will see a spruce garland with white tulips on a table decorated for a New Year's Eve party.

Tips

If a garland is going to hang curved, you can tie it in such a manner that the branches on each side of the arc curve toward the lowest point of the curve.

A garland that is going to frame a door should be tied in three parts, which will hang separately. First hang two vertical pieces with the points of the branches facing down, then add a horizontal piece on the top. The top piece can be made with branches going in two different directions from a center point. The center joint is then concealed with sprigs.

If you want a dense, round, and chubby garland, wrap the wires so that all side branches are pressed into the main branch.

A string of small, electric lights attached to the garland will help convey the luminous warmth of the holidays.

Christmas Tree Ideas

Why decorate the deep green, living spruce with glitter and finery? Fresh flowers and other materials from nature suit it better. Make sure to collect pinecones, lichen, and moss earlier in the year.

Decorating Ideas

... with hyacinths

Hang test tubes with flowers in them directly on the tree. At a florist's, you can buy test tubes with holes at the top for attaching a wire for hanging. You can also use glass containers with wide openings, where the hanging wire is secured under the opening.

... with beech husks

Wrap the stem wire tightly around the stem of each husk. Continuously unwrap the stem wire from the spool as you attach each one to the "vine," and then repeat at even spacing until your chain is the length you desire.

... with hyacinth bulbs

Wrap moss around a clump of earth to form a pouch to hold the bulb. Make an outer "frame" of stem wire to hold the pouch and use it to hang from the tree, allowing the top of the bulb to be visible.

49

. . . with tiny poinsettias

Remove the poinsettia from its flowerpot, place moss around the clump of potting soil, and attach the moss with stem wire. Make a hanging wire of the same stem wire. You can use the pot for the smallest plants. Wrap the whole pot in moss and attach it with stem wire. Spray the moss occasionally with water to keep slightly damp.

. . . with baby pinecones

Wrap stem wire a few times around the baby cones. Repeat with evenly spaced distances until the chain is long enough.

. . . with tulips

Fill test tubes with large, white tulips and hang them from the tree.

. . . with larch cones

Wrap stem wire a few times around the larch cone. Repeat at even intervals until the chain is long enough.

Natural Elements Holiday Balls

Moss balls

Place a small fistful of moss on a larger patch of flat moss, shape all into a ball, and wrap with stem wire. You can also use a dry floral foam ball covered with moss to create the same effect.

Lichen balls

Form a ball of moss and wrap lichen around it. Leafy lichen is excellent. You can also use reindeer lichen (Cladonia stellaris), or any other lichen. In this instance, you can utilize a dry floral foam ball.

Conifer cone balls

Snippets of greenery from spruce, fir, or juniper, together with conifer cones, can become the most beautiful Christmas balls. Wrap with stem wire.

Balls on a stem

Fasten the ball on the top of a twisted, stiff metal wire, which has been attached to a lead base or something similar. You can cover the metal wire with floral tape.

55

Miniature Birch Bark Trees

These simple, miniature birch bark trees can be used as a charming addition for a table, or they can be hung as decorations on a Christmas tree.

The moss trees can be found on page 82.

Instructions

* Scrape away loose patches on the white side of the bark.
* Glue two large pieces together, white side against white side, place heavy books or other weights on top of bark so it drys flat. Let them dry for a few days.
* Draw the tree pattern on the bark, as shown on page 127. You can utilize the bark more efficiently if you place the pattern in the opposite direction of the previous drawing.
* Cut out the trees and mount them together.

Tip

The bark from an older birch tree may be more dense than that of a younger tree. If you use the thicker bark you may not need to glue two pieces together: this is recommended to provide greater stability when using thinner birch bark.

Materials

* birch bark
* slow-drying glue

Baby Pinecone Trees

Gather the pinecones when they are bright green and immature (usually in the spring), and let them dry in an airy place. You will be surprised by how much they shrink, yet the shape remains, and the color becomes a golden brown with a touch of gray green.

Materials

* cone-shaped floral foam
* small pinecones
* hot-glue gun and glue sticks

Instructions

* With a glue gun, apply glue over a small area of the floral foam.
* Glue on the pinecones, with bottoms of the cones next to tops as you build your rows. Start with the largest pinecones at the bottom, and work your way around the form before starting the next row.
* At the end, glue the small pinecone stems in the spaces between the pinecones.

Tips

Don't forget to remove the glue threads at the end!

Party Table Decorations

Twig & Flower Table Decoration

If you have a bundle of nice sticks, you can quickly set an inviting table. Arrange the twigs like a ribbon in the middle of the table, and place silk flowers, or another type of artificial flowers with large heads, on top of the twigs. Decorate with tea lights and an ivy vine. The guests are guaranteed to notice the simple, refined table decoration.

Instructions

* Cut the twigs into short sticks.
* Arrange the twigs in a line in the center of the table, and place the glass candleholders nicely among them.
* Arrange the flowers loosely on top of the twigs, and let the ivy snake elegantly from flower to flower.

Tips

During Advent it is fitting to decorate with purple orchids and purple candles. In the fall, you can decorate with rowan berries or other berries, and lichen, stones, and conifer cones. In the summer, you can add seashells and other materials from the beach. If you want to use flowers that need water, you can place them in small, plastic water holders with rubber tops, which you hide under the twigs.

Materials

* twigs
* short glasses for tea lights
* silk flowers with big heads
* ivy

63

Vines

A decorated vine that lies elegantly upon the table and winds its way between glasses and plates is a beautiful sight. There is almost no end to what you can wrap around a vine made of a soft, pliable, climbing plant. Ivy is excellent as a point of departure. You can emphasize the evening's theme with your choice of materials. The vine can be more or less richly decorated. Only your imagination limits the possibilities!

Materials

* ivy, Virginia creeper or other pliable climbing plants
* larch cones, alder cones, flax, feathers, wheat sheaves, flowers from climbing hydrangeas or other types of dry decorations
* tulips or similar fresh flowers
* stem wire

Instructions

* Attach all dry and preserved materials with stem wire at appropriate intervals and in the order you prefer. You can do this many days before the party.
* Just before the party begins, place the vine on the table, add tulip heads or other flowers to the vine with stem wire.

es that need a lot of water can be placed
water holders with rubber tops. Cover the
der with a green leaf.

ou are going to decorate the vine with many
erials, it is smart to attach the stem wire
he thin end and wrap the wire toward the
er end of the vine as you work. You can
flowers and natural materials as you go.

materials in your garden or in forests.
d heads and spent flowers from
rangeas and bridal veils, for example, give
ume. Lingonberry bushes or other heathers
a nice green color if you make the vine
m branches without leaves. When using
tiple dry materials, you don't need a lot
resh flowers.

not wrap the stem wire around the vine
tightly.

ine can also be hung as a garland around
altar for a wedding, over an entrance, or
a spiral around a column.

Flower & Moss Table Decoration

If the table you are decorating is so narrow that common tabletop decorations do not fit, you can be creative: use a small strip of chicken wire, bend it by hand to form "waves", slip test tubes through the mesh, and place a single flower and some grass straws into each test tube. Between the top of the waves, you can decorate with candles or whatever you wish.

Materials

* chicken wire
* test tubes
* flowers and other decorations
* candles

Instructions

* Cut a long strip of chicken wire with wire cutters.
* Bend the chicken wire into a long series of waves, preferably of different heights, and let it lay flat on the table.
* Slip test tubes through the mesh into the waves, and on the flat areas you can put other decorations.

Tips

A strand of small electric lights along with the table garland will enhance the party mood. If the table is very wide or square, you can make four short garlands and place them in a square in the middle of the table.

If you exchange the white tulips with red flowers or rose hips, you will have a beautiful party garland for your holiday table.

Tulip & Spruce Table Garland

On page 44 you can see an example of a fir garland attached to a stair railing. Here we have used a spruce garland as a decoration in the middle of the table for a New Year's Eve party. By adding white tulips, the decoration becomes both simple and elegant.

Instructions

* Cut the side branches off the main branch if you want a narrow garland, or use the whole branch if you want the garland to be wide and large.
* Place one branch partially on top of another branch, and wrap them together with spool wire. Place new branches on top of the others, carefully arranging them to offset each other. Wrap. Make sure that the spool wire only wraps around the main branch in a way that does not push the side branches too close to the main branch.
* Hide the end point, which terminates the garland, with sprigs that are wrapped in the opposite direction.
* Slip in tulips, evenly spacing them. The garland may be quite exuberant for a party table. Tulips which have been in water for a long time manage quite well for a whole evening without water holders.
* You may decorate the garland with spruce cones in addition to the tulips.

68

A Traditional Table Arrangement

Materials

* a shallow dish
* floral foam
* flowers and greenery

By a traditional arrangement, I mean one where the flowers are set in the shape of a fan in a dish with moist floral form. It is a classic shape and can be used at any occasion. For this design, I have used warm, glowing holiday colors and traditional holiday flowers.

Instructions

* Press a moist piece of floral foam lightly into an appropriate, shallow dish. The foam should sit about one inch above the rim of the dish.
* Start with the greenery, which should extend out of the dish onto the table. You can make the decoration as long as you wish, depending upon the width of the table.
* When most of the green materials have been put in place, arrange the flowers in a harmonious composition.
* Cover any visible foam with moss or lichen.

Tips

Preferably, use slim, elegant juniper twigs in the long direction, and shorter sprigs across.

Lingonberry branches can be used throughout a great part of the year. They create variations in the green color and texture.

Collect the flowers in groups. Do not use too many colors or types of flowers. The completed design should be highest in the middle and slope down and out.

Unique Horn Table Decoration

If you can get hold of horns from sheep, goats, or other animals, you won't need a long time to decorate the table! Horns are hollow, and a green leaf and a flower inside are enough to make a fun arrangement. If you use the same flowers as in the main decoration, it can be a nice way of extending the decoration without needing so many additional flowers.

Instructions

* If the horn has not been cleaned, you have to first boil out the marrow and hang the horn to dry. Work outside, because the process smells strongly.
* If the horn has a leakage, plug it with waterproof glue.
* Fill the horn with water, and place something green and one flower or more in the opening.

Tips

If the flower's stem is short, place the flower in a water holder with a rubber top, and set it in the horn's opening. Make sure that green leaves are concealing the rubber top.

Materials

* a hollow horn that will sit with stability on the table
* some flowers and greenery — for example, a leaf, juniper, spruce, or cedar sprigs, etc.
* waterproof glue

Materials

* juniper branches
* amaryllis flowers
* lichen, corky fungi, or other natural materials
* floral foam and a dish

Fanciful Decoration with Amaryllis

A striking arrangement doesn't need many elements: one amaryllis in the center, one corky fungus, and a little lichen. Add three red dogwood twigs, which pick up the red color in the flower, and green juniper and lingonberry sprigs. You do not need more.

Instructions

* Moisten the floral foam and place it into dish, then put all the green materials in the foam.
* Stick the flowers in front and decorate with other natural materials.

Tips

The amaryllis should be placed in its own water holder. Flowers with stiff stems can be stuck directly into the foam.

74

Amaryllis Tree

Amaryllises are fabulous winter flowers, both in pots and cut. They become an elegant eye-catcher when wrapped tightly together, so that the big flower bells create a ball.

Instructions

* Tie a pretty rope around the flower stems at the top under the bells, and wrap the rope, tightly spaced, until it covers about two inches of the stems.
* Finish by wrapping the rope in moderate spirals into the vase, and fasten it with a loose knot at the bottom around the stems.

Tips

Let the bouquet stand in a narrow and slightly heavy vase, so that it does not become unbalanced.

Here I have concealed the vase with sticks and topped it with lichen. See instructions on page 109.

Materials

* amaryllises
* rope
* vase
* several sticks, approximately the same size
* lichen

Oval-Shaped Hawthorn "Pillow"

The modest and fragile Lenten rose that I use in this design reminds me of the wood anemone, which makes a brief appearance in spring. The Lenten rose also vanishes from the markets around the New Year, so enjoy it while you can — preferably on an oval hawthorn pillow. Other flowers that work well with this arrangement are azaleas and cyclamens.

Older hawthorn trees have fascinating and gnarled twigs, often covered with lichen in different hues. If you discover a dead hawthorn tree, you should make sure that you get branches from it. However, other branches with strong characteristics can also be used.

Materials

* hawthorn branches
* thick floral wire
* spool wire
* stem wire
* Lenten roses, azaleas, cyclamen, or other flowers
* platter, a bit smaller your oval shape

Instructions

* Form two equally large rings by twisting several floral wires together to create the oval-shape forms. The depicted pillow is approximately 15" x 10".
* In one of the rings, make a mesh network of floral wires crisscrossing each other (see photo on next page). Eventually, you can reduce the size of the openings in the mesh with spool wire. The mesh can be quite open because the small hawthorn branches will, after you place them, create a tight network.

(continues on the next page)

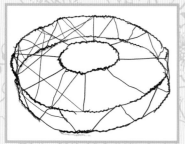

* Attach the two rings to each other with approximately a two-inch gap by wrapping a thick floral wire a few times around the top ring, and thereafter a few times around the bottom ring, and then again, wrapping it a couple of times around the top ring. Repeat this "zigzag" pattern around the whole shape. Don't worry if the framework is not perfect; the imbalance or crookedness can be adjusted when you start arranging the twigs.

* Attach the hawthorn twigs to the frame so that as much of the floral wire is covered as possible. Each twig is attached at two points with stem wire, either to the frame or to other twigs. Lock in place with 4-5 twists. Cut off the wire ends. Complete the top surface before you start to cover the sidewall.

* Place the hawthorn pillow over a platter with water. Decorate the pillow with flowers and leaves as desired. Do not use too many decorations — let the beautiful hawthorn branches shine on their own.

Tips

You can adjust the shape to fit any platter you have.

Moss & Berry Trees

Materials

* chicken wire
* moss
* silver-, gold-, or bronze-colored stem wire
* spool wire
* votive candles

Moss trees, which can be placed directly on the table-cloth, create a forest mood for the holiday table. Make the trees in different sizes, and place them grouped, two or three together. Decorate with natural materials or let them stand without. Tiny votive candles enhance the mood. You can make these trees either with chicken wire (see page 127) or cone-shaped floral foam.

Instructions

* Follow the instructions on page 127 for making the cone-shaped form out of chicken wire. Then, follow the instructions in the next bullet point.
* Bend the chicken wire into a cone shape, and fasten the two long sides to each other with spool wire.
* Bend in the bottom of the mesh.
* Place moss all around the mesh and wrap with stem wire in parallel circles (spirals) toward the bottom.
* Finish the wrapping at the bottom by "sewing" the stem wire through the chicken wire along the whole bottom edge.

Miniature birch bark trees are found on page 57.

Candlesticks
and Vases

Antler Candlestick

Materials

* one adequately sized antler
* one or more candle-holders with spikes
* natural materials for decoration — for example, pinecones, lichen, club moss, or fir club moss
* spool wire or stem wire
* drill

If, on your trips in forests or into fields, you find an antler that the mice have not had time to gnaw asunder, you have to take it with you. It can become a unique candlestick!

Instructions

* Drill one or more holes in the antler.
* Press a candleholder into the hole(s), and cut any visible spikes on the underside.
* Attach natural materials using stem wire, and fasten the wire to the spike right under the candle dish.

Delightful Candlesticks with Apples

Apples paired with burning candles belong to Christmas! And the apples aren't only for eating. Here they have become surprising and rustic candlesticks. As a base, I have used a charming, old, iron monk's pan, but a large, flat stone can do the same job.

Instructions

* Apply a medium-size dab of hot glue to the base.
* Immediately press the apple down onto the hot glue.
* Press the candleholder with a spike into the apple.
* Decorate with some fresh greens — for example, club moss or lichen.

Tips

You can use an old frying pan as a base.

For Easter, green apples and yellow candles look lovely.

Materials

* red apples
* iron monk's pan (or another base)
* hot-glue gun and glue sticks
* candleholders with long spikes
* candles
* club moss or lichen

Materials

* one piece of wire cloth
  (the same height as the
  floral foam)
* large-size floral foam
* staple gun and staples
* many large conifer cones
* larch cone twigs
* test tubes or water holders
* pan-melt glue pot and
  glue- or hot-glue gun and
  glue sticks
* stem wire

The conifer cone vase can also be made into a candlestick. You exchange the test tubes for candleholders with long spikes and glue the cone scales closely up the candleholders.

Conifer Cone Vase

If you give yourself the time to make a large conifer cone vase, you will not regret it. Handle it carefully, and it can last forever. You can place the floral foam on the top and make one hole for flowers or lay it down and make three holes. You can also glue together several pieces of foam and cut them into any shape you want.

Instructions

* If your wire cloth has a wide mesh like in the photograph on the opposite page, you may want to color the floral foam with a marker before going any further, to avoid it showing through. Attach the wire cloth to the floral foam with staples and then fasten a few larch cone twigs with stem wire.
* Make the hole (or holes) in the foam and then press one or more test tubes or water holders into the holes.
* Using the large cones, strip off the scales and cut them at an angle at the bottom (see the photograph below). It is best to cut the scales with as sharp a point as possible, to avoid crumbling the foam.
* For the next step, you can use either a pan-melt glue pot or a hot-glue gun. Dip the sharpened end of each scale in the glue and quickly stick it into the foam, or apply dabs of hot glue and do the same. Begin at the top and work downward, densely applying the scales.
* At the end, fill any unwanted spaces with smaller cone scales.

90

Materials

* open beech husks, preferably light brown
* birch bark
* floral foam
* glue pan or hot-glue gun
* water holder
* marker

Tips

The ball can be hung as a year-round decoration. Make a hook for hanging by sticking a bent floral wire through the ball and the piece of bark, and bend the ends of the wire to each side at the bottom.

Beech Husk Ball

When the beech tree loses its husks, the ground below is covered with them. Gather the husks before they become full of dark spots from rain and moisture. Dry and store the husks; they are beautiful raw materials for decorations. You can also make the husk ball into a candlestick. If so, the water holder is replaced by a candleholder with a long spike, and the husks are glued closely to the candleholder.

Instructions

* If you are using ball-shaped floral foam, cut a piece off the bottom so that it sits stably.
* You can color the foam black with a marker, then it will not show through between the husks.
* Cut a round piece of flat birch bark and glue it to the bottom of the foam.
* Press the water holder into a hole in the foam. The more water a flower needs, the larger the size of the water container you must use.
* Dip the husk stem in glue (from a pan-melt glue pot or a hot-glue gun), and stick it quickly into the floral foam. The husks should be placed closely so that the foam does not show.

Bottle Decoration

This rustic wine bottle with its strong green color can become a beautiful vase for certain flowers with long stems, such as anthuriums, as shown. Use three bottles, and you can make an elegant arrangement. Use the same type of flowers for each bottle, and link the bottles with twigs or grasses. Here I have decorated one of the bottles with a tiny anthurium, a few small alder cones, some feathers, and paper lichen set in a self-attaching mini floral foam.

Instructions

* To assemble the self-attaching mini floral foam, hot glue the foam onto the bottle and saturate it with water.
* Decorate the foam with small-size flowers, lichen, juniper, alder cones, or anything that will fit the occasion. Stick the stems directly into the foam, and glue other items.

Tips

A bottle of wine, given as a hostess gift, is an even nicer if you adorn it with a small, personal decoration.

A gift will distinguish itself, if it has a mini decoration of flowers or other natural materials attached to the wrapping paper.

Materials

* one or several empty wine bottles
* self-attaching mini floral foam piece, about 1" in diameter
* dogwood twigs or grasses
* small-size cones, flowers, etc.
* hot-glue gun and glue sticks

95

Twig Vase

Materials

* twigs of mixed lengths
* test tubes or other water holders
* rubber bands
* rope
* hot-glue gun and glue sticks
* flowers

A collection of twigs of different sizes, placed around three test tubes or other glass water holders becomes an artistic vase.

Instructions

* Collect many twigs, preferably of different sizes and colors. The twigs should be quite straight. Green and red dogwood, lime tree, and maple are good examples. Use the thinnest part of the branch with a thickness of about ⅓ inch. Cut the twigs into sticks of mixed lengths, and gather them with two strong rubber bands.
* Using the rubber-band method above, you can stick three test tubes (use test tubes that are approximately 4 to 5 inches tall) between the sticks, and then tie the rope around the sticks at the bottom, cut off the rubber band, and tie again higher up. If you are using another water holder, you can attach your mixed-length twigs directly to the outside of the glass vase with hot glue and forego the rubber-band method. Tie with rope as described.
* You can add new twigs or tighten the ropes as the twigs dry and shrink.

Tips

If you use completely fresh twigs, they will release a lot of moisture in the beginning. Be aware that mold may develop at the base, move the vase frequently to prevent this.

When all the sticks have dried, you can freshen up the vase by replacing some of them with fresh sticks. This occurs especially with the colored twigs, which fade after a while.

If you have to exchange the test tubes, replace one at a time; if you remove all at once, there is a chance that the twigs will fall apart.

Bark Vase

Here's a different take on a vase: a piece of bark with test tubes mounted on it, placed in a ceramic container. Choose the ceramic container first, and then look for bark that will fit inside it. Sometimes I have found the perfectly sized piece of bark, but occasionally I have had to trim the bark to fit. With a few simple materials, you can make a creative (and durable) decoration that will suit every season with a simple change of flowers.

Materials

* a large piece of stiff bark
* a ceramic container
* test tubes
* spool wire or stem wire
* orchids or other flowers

Instructions

* If the piece of bark is too large, trim it so that it will fit in the ceramic container.
* Drill two small holes close to each other through the bark, thread spool wire or stem wire through the holes from behind, twist the wire ends together a few times on the front, and fasten the wire around the test tube. Attach each test tube to the bark in two places.

Tips

If you use a piece of bark that is not too stiff but can stand by itself, you can attach it to a block of floral foam. Place it in a ceramic container, cover it with moss, and keep it moist.

98

Winter Decorations

Orchids & Bark

If you discover a rotted tree in the forest, study the bark.
Has it loosened from the trunk? Is it unusual, with deep
grooves, or covered with fine lichen? Perhaps you can spot
a network of grooves on the inside, where the bark beetles
have burrowed. Gather some large pieces — they can be
the start of a sculptural decoration.

Instructions

* Evaluate how the bark can be used. Standing?
  Lying? Upside down? Back to front? Choose the
  most interesting position.
* Place a glass dish or a vase, possibly with a pin frog,
  behind the bark, and arrange the flowers in this. Let
  the flowers poke out through slots in the bark.

Materials

* thick bark
* pin frog
* glass dish or vase
* spool wire
* orchids or other flowers

Tips

If the piece of bark is in the process of splitting,
you can keep it together by using spool wire to tie
the pieces.

Hyacinths

There are many types of containers that can be fun points of departure for decoration. Here, I have used an old wooden box that was left over from a beehive installation. Time has given it a charming patina that provides character, and the thin, differently sized pieces of slate present another texture inside the box and help to support the blooming hyacinth bulbs. If your container is not waterproof, you may need a plastic insert or something similar to protect it from water damage.

Instructions

* Place slate pieces between the edges of the box so tension holds them upright. Divide the spaces with more slate pieces placed perpendicularly.
* Place bulbs closely together in all the spaces, so that the slate is supported.
* Cover the spaces between the bulbs with moss.

Tips

Spray the bulbs occasionally, but do not let them stand in water.

If you want to use cut flowers, you can place pieces of floral foam between the slate pieces. Cover the moist foam with moss or lichen, and press the flowers into them.

Materials

* a wooden or metal box, a tray, a platter, or a ceramic container of good enough height to hold the bulbs and moss (plus, you may need a plastic insert if your container is not waterproof)
* slate pieces of different heights and sizes
* hyacinth bulbs (or another not-too-tall flowering bulb)
* moss
* floral foam (if you use cut flowers)

Begonias & Seasonal Elements

The warm, rosy-pink blooms of wax begonias are a beautiful complement to the aged wooden trough that I used for this decoration — but they will easily do the same for almost any container that you might have. Moss, pinecones, and lichen are used to fill the trough.

Instructions

* If your container is not waterproof, cover the inside with thick plastic. Place the plant, without the pot, in the trough.
* Arrange the other materials in groups around the plant.

Tips

Spray the lichen and moss now and then to preserve their freshness.

Materials

* a platter or trough
* moss, lichen, corky fungi, stones, or conifer cones
* wax begonia or another plant
* plastic insert

Twig Pot Cover

Cover boring flowerpots with natural materials —
for example, a web of larch twigs.

Materials

* thin larch twigs or
  other types of wood
* spool wire

Instructions

* Cut the twigs into sticks of approximately the
  same length.
* Weave the sticks together into a long "row" with two
  long spool wires (see photograph at right). Bend each
  spool wire and place a little bundle of sticks farthest
  within the bend. Lock the sticks in place by twisting
  the ends of the wires tightly around each other. Thereafter, place a new bundle next to the first and tighten
  again. Continue until the mat is long enough that you
  can cover the pot. Make a cylinder out of the mat and
  fasten the ends of the wires to each other.

Tips

Instead of bundles of thin sticks, you can weave together one thin twig and one fat twig. You can use all
kinds of twigs, as long as they are somewhat straight
and of the same approximate length.

Flat moss wrapped around a pot is another simple
way of concealing it. Be sure to thoroughly dry the
moss before wrapping.

109

Star of David

Materials

* dry persicaria stalks
* spool wire
* ivy
* flowers
* drill

Persicaria (also known as knotweed or pinkweed) is an annoying invasive plant, but to a floral designer, it presents opportunities for natural arrangements. The joints on its stalks act as waterproof casings, and this feature can be put to great use. Here, the stalks of the persicaria are formed into a Star of David and the casings act like vases for fresh flowers.

Instructions

* Cut six equally long and approximately equally thick pieces from persicaria stalks.
* Fasten them together into two triangles with the help of spool wire (see "How to tie two branches together," page 9).
* Then fasten the two triangles together using spool wire, so that you get six points.
* Make a hanging loop for the star using the spool wire.
* Carefully drill holes in the stalks, as high as possible in the waterproof casings of the "standing" stalks, and anywhere at the top of the horizontal stalks.
* Decorate the Star of David with ivy or similar green vines
* Thereafter, decorate with any flowers you wish. Here, I have used white flowers from an azalea, and on page 100 you will see the star decorated with flowers from a pink wax begonia.

Tips

There are many types of flowers that will work well. The only requirement is that the stem be sufficiently long and robust so that it can tolerate being pushed through the holes in the stalks.

Pinecone Trees

What would a holiday decoration be without pinecones? Luckily, they are not in short supply and can be found almost everywhere (or purchased from a craft or hobby store). This design, Pinecone Trees, uses primarily smaller to mid-size cones, so be sure to collect a lot.

Materials
* pinecones and pins
* floral wire
* staples
* cone-shaped floral foam
* glue in a glue pan
* flat moss
* sprigs of mistletoe, catkins, or lichen

Instructions
* Pin the pinecones (see page 9).
* Cut off the top of the cone-shaped foam, and cover the whole piece with flat moss; attach it with greening pins.
* Once the moss is completely attached, gather the pinned pinecones and as you work, dip each one in the glue pan and then stick through the moss and into the foam.
* Start at the bottom, and cover the foam densely with pinecones.
* Finish with one pinecone at the top.

Tips
You can buy floral foam cones in many sizes. A still life of pinecone trees in several sizes can be used as a nice table decoration.

Decorate the trees with sprigs of mistletoe, catkins, or lichen.

Moss Heart

A chubby moss heart is much easier to make than you think! You can use the form year-round and on many holidays. Occasionally lay a fresh, new layer of flat moss on top of the old.

Materials

* chicken wire
* flat moss
* very thin stem wire
* spool wire

Instructions

* Cut out two hearts from chicken wire, a little larger than you want the finished heart.
* "Sew" the two hearts together with spool wire, or bend them together along the edges, and pull them away from each other so that there is "air" between them.
* Lay moss on top, and wrap it securely with thin stem wire as shown in the photograph.

Tips

The larger the size of the
chicken wire mesh, the
thicker the flower stems
you can use. Alternatively,
you can enlarge the holes
in a small mesh by using
your wire cutters.

Instead of wool, which I
have used along the edge
of the chicken wire, you
can wrap the edges with
bear moss. A thick rope
can also become a nice
frame. If you can get hold
of feathers, they can make
a light and elegant frame
for the mat. You have
many possibilities, so
use your imagination!

You can also use heather,
lingonberry greenery, fir,
or any other durable
greenery for the mat.

Sculptural White Lilies & Noble Fir

The suspended mat of noble fir sprigs holds the Amazon lilies in place (narcissus, tulips, or any other long-stemmed flower will also work). When the flowers are placed in a row over a larger area, the expression becomes quite different than if they are placed tightly together in an ordinary vase.

Instructions

* Cut a piece of chicken wire a little larger than the box you are going to use. Use wire cutters and cut so that the sharp points are not sticking out.
* Place wool along the edge of your chicken wire and wrap it with stem wire.
* When you are done covering the edges, bend them down.
* Weave in short sprigs of noble spruce to create the mat, and leave some to hang over the edges.
* To create the structure that will hold the mat, cut several twigs of the same thickness and length. Attach one twig at each corner of the mat using spool wire, and let the twigs stick up over the mat to form a point (see the photograph at left). You can also attach a few twigs on the diagonal between the corners for stiffening.
* Push the flowers through the mat and the chicken wire down into the box.

Materials

* a box, a tray, or a platter (whatever you choose must have some height at the edges)
* wire cutters
* chicken wire
* wool, moss, rope, or something similar that will work for wrapping along the edge of the chicken wire
* twigs
* spool wire
* stem wire
* noble spruce sprigs
* lilies, narcissus, tulips, or any long-stemmed flowers

Woven Curtain with Amaryllis

A decorative and transparent curtain of flowers, sticks, and spool wire makes any room ready for a party! Christmas or New Years is the high season for amaryllises and you can use them to create this "curtain" of flowers. Try the snow-white ones or any of the other beautiful color options from this lovely holiday flower. Hung upside down with water in the hollow stem, the amaryllis will keep its bloom for a long time.

Materials

* two long, thin tree branches
* spool wire (green-colored wire is used here)
* dogwood twigs or other thin twigs, for stiffening
* rope
* drill

Tips

If you want to decorate the curtain with flowers that do not have a hollow stem, you can fasten test tubes to the web. Then you can hang them upright.

The bottom branch must be heavy enough and have tension to stretch the spool wire.

Instructions

* Drill a hole near the end of each branch, and fasten rope through the holes, so that the distance between the two branches stays even. The length of the rope determines the height of the curtain.
* Hang the top branch horizontally. You can, as needed, adjust the length of the rope between the two branches to balance the curtain.
* Drill narrow holes through each branch, spaced about 4" apart.
* Fasten the spool wire through the hole in the top, and fasten the wire in the corresponding hole at the bottom. Tighten the wire. Fasten vertical wires through all the holes.
* Fasten some wires at an angle through the same holes.
* It is smart to weave in some additional twigs to stiffen the curtain (here, I have used dogwood). Some of them should be fastened to the branches, and some to the ropes.
* Fasten the amaryllises upside down with spool wire. Remember to fill the stems with water.

Little Twig Globe with Tulips

With simple materials, you can make a globe-shaped twig form into which you can thread fresh flowers. The contrast between the gray-brown coarse twigs and the soft, bent stems of the white tulips is enchanting.

Instructions

* Make two or more rings from floral wire. Add more layers of floral wires, wrapped around each other to make stiff rings.
* Fasten the rings together with spool wire, so they form a globe.
* Attach the twigs to the globe, using spool wire. Once covered, attach more twigs to the already fastened ones. Fasten each twig at least twice, keeping the globe airy and transparent.
* To stabilize, attach the globe to the handles of the pot using spool wire. Fill the pot with water, and decorate the globe with the tulips.

Tips

In addition to tulips, the long-stemmed gloriosa lily will work well in this decoration. It is helpful if the stems are pliable.

Materials

* distinctive, fresh twigs
* thick floral wire
* spool wire
* heavy pot
* flowers as desired

121

Big Twig Globe with Candle

This globe is easy to make, but still spectacular! It can be hung by an entrance or placed in a heavy iron pot on stairs or a bench. Regardless, it welcomes guests warmly.

Materials

* two or more stiff metal rings made from spool wire
* spool wire
* floral wire
* bendable twigs, preferably covered with lichen
* fir sprigs and pinecones
* heavy pot
* candleholders, lead "hood," and candle (if desired)

Instructions

* Make two or more rings from spool wire. Add more layers of wire, wrapped around each other to make stiff rings.
* Fasten the rings together with spool wire, so they form a globe.
* Using floral wire, attach the twigs, fir sprigs, and pinecones to the globe. Once covered, attach more twigs to the already fastened ones. Fasten each twig at least twice, keeping the globe airy and transparent.
* If desired, place a candleholder at the bottom of the pot. Make a "hood" of lead and hang it from the top of the globe, directly over where the flame will be. Place a hurricane lamp shade over the candle to protect it from the wind.
* To stabilize, attach the globe to the pot using spool wire.

Tips

Decorate the globe with some "everlasting" greenery — for example, club moss or noble spruce. You can also decorate with chains of rose hips or alder cones.

Bowed Twigs & Anthurium Decoration

This simple decoration is based upon the shape of an arc made from hazel tree twigs. Together with a simple anthurium, some moss, lichen, a pinecone, and a bunch of twigs, it makes a luxurious statement. Use freshly sprouted or leafless hazel twigs.

Instructions

* Use a shallow, low-sided, waterproof container, and place a moistened piece of floral foam in the bottom.
* Cut the red dogwood stems at an angle, as shown in the photograph at bottom right.
* Insert the log hazel twigs on each side of the foam, and tie them together with stem wire to create an arc over the decoration. Add several twigs to balance the arc if it is crooked.

Tips

Keep the flower inside the arc. Both birch and dogwood also work well for the arc. Larch twigs with a few cones are always decorative! Pick twigs, place them in water, and sprout the leaves inside to use in this piece.

Materials

* shallow, waterproof container
* moistened piece of floral foam
* long hazel tree twigs with catkins, plus fir sprigs, club moss, and reindeer moss
* anthurium flower
* red dogwood stems
* stem wire

Tall Twigs with Anthurium & Calla Lily

Twigs of all kinds, bare or with buds ready to burst, can do wonders for a decoration. The twigs give the flower character, and the flower makes the twigs come alive.

Materials

* small pot and pin frog that will fit inside
* a few tall twigs; include one or two with buds
* greenery, such as magnolia leaves
* a calla lily, anthurium, and star-of-Bethlehem or narcissus
* lichen

Instructions

* Place the pin frog in the small pot. Insert one or two twigs, then add greenery and the flowers of your choice. Add the lichen as a final touch.
* When the decoration is done, or while you are making it, adjust the twigs with regard to height and placement, so that the decoration is harmonious and balanced.
* Remove unnecessary side branches from the twigs.

Tips

Here, I have used a vigorous anthurium, which is resting upon a bed of magnolia leaves and lichen. A calla lily and a star-of-Bethlehem rise high above the decoration. Notice how the top of the calla lily and the outer points of the twigs point toward the center and pull the decoration together.

126

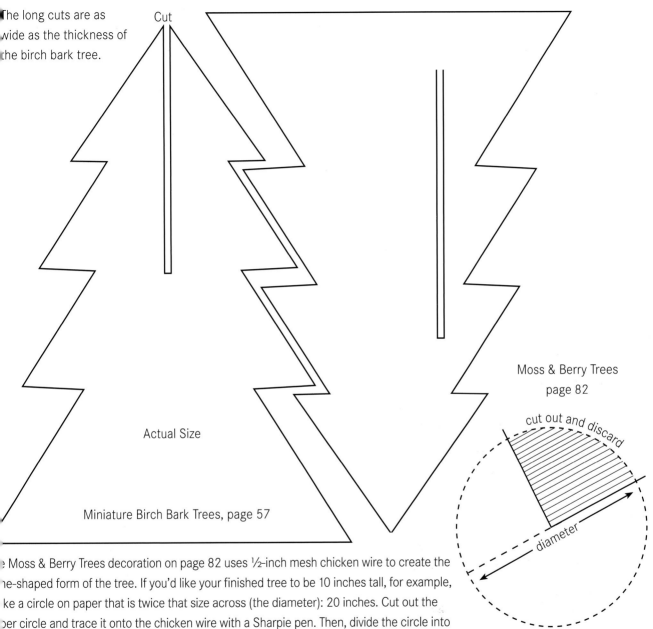

The long cuts are as wide as the thickness of the birch bark tree.

Cut

Actual Size

Miniature Birch Bark Trees, page 57

Moss & Berry Trees
page 82

cut out and discard

diameter

The Moss & Berry Trees decoration on page 82 uses ½-inch mesh chicken wire to create the cone-shaped form of the tree. If you'd like your finished tree to be 10 inches tall, for example, make a circle on paper that is twice that size across (the diameter): 20 inches. Cut out the paper circle and trace it onto the chicken wire with a Sharpie pen. Then, divide the circle into four equal pie shapes and mark on the chicken wire. Cut your wire circle with wire cutters and then cut out one "piece of pie" and discard. What you are left with is what you'll use to form the cone shape. Wearing gloves, wrap the remaining circle into a cone shape and use either spool wire to secure it or bend the chicken wire and attach it to itself. Make any adjustments to the bottom of the cone so it sits in a stable manner. Add the moss as directed on page 82.